The garage of Mr R. O. Darling at Eardisley, Herefordshire, in the 1930s.

THE COUNTRY GARAGE

Llyn E. Morris

Shire Publications Ltd

CONTENTS

Published in 2010 by Shire Publications Ltd, Midland House, West Way, Botley, Oxford OX2 0PH, UK. Copyright © 1985 by the estate of the late Llyn E. Morris. First published 1985, reprinted 1995 and 2010. Shire Library 129. ISBN-13: 978 0 85263 711 1.

Printed in China through Worldprint Ltd.

British Library Cataloguing in Publication data: Morris, Llyn E. The country garage. — (Shire Library; 129). 1. Automobiles — Service stations — Great Britain — History. 2. Great Britain — Rural conditions. I. Title 338.4'7629286'0941 TL153. ISBN 0-85263-711-X.

COVER: *A detail from a Shell lorry advertisement of 1925, designed by D. C. Fouqueray and reproduced by kind permission of Shell UK Ltd.*

A STORY WITHOUT WORDS

'Among the characteristics . . . essentially British is the tendency to receive almost any innovation . . . with some distrust which shows itself in satirical criticism; to be followed soon afterwards by the acceptance of the accomplished fact and complete approval,' wrote 'Punch' — here sceptical of the car's mechanism.

MEMORANDUM.

From . .

O. SIMPSON,

Agent for the

Daimler Cars & Launch Motors,

Lubricating Oils, Grease,

PETROL & IGNITION TUBES ALWAYS IN STOCK,

Prices on application.   Repairs at reasonable charges.

Memorandum slip printed for a grandfather of the author's wife. He gave up farming to become an early Daimler agent and is pictured at the tiller of the car.

ORIGINS AND GROWTH

The first motorcars appeared on the roads of Great Britain in 1895 and in the following year the Locomotives on Highways Act removed some of the restrictions encumbering them. But 'Liberty Day', 14th November 1896, when pioneer motorists celebrated their new freedom, merely marked the start of a long obstacle course of legal and technical difficulties to be overcome in a rural Britain attuned to the horse and the railway.

Wealth and sporting instincts were necessary qualifications for the motorist, to which technical ability was often added. Journeys across country needed careful planning, for he had to purchase his fuel at ironmongers or oil shops, as well as carrying some with him. When the vehicle broke down, he or his chauffeur had to repair it. If another motorist chanced by, the newcomer would (according to contemporary etiquette) render assistance. However, if the car could not be repaired on the spot, the defeated motorist had to suffer the indignity of a horse tow to the nearest establishment which had the tools, skill and material to aid him.

This was often a cycle shop, which itself might have grown out of an ironmongery business. The cycle had become increasingly popular in the 1890s and the trade enjoyed a boom in 1896 and 1897 when fashionable society took up the machine. When this fad ended, enterprising shopkeepers saw that the motor vehicle could supplant it. Moreover, the cycle companies themselves were diversifying into motor-vehicle manufacture and there was therefore a ready-forged link between manufacturer and agent. In this way the shop owner moved via the motorcycle (possibly tricycle) and car hire to car sales and repairs. Lord Nuffield, in Oxford, furnishes the finest example of such a progression.

Not all motor businesses grew from cycle shops. Coachbuilding had been carried on since the improvements of the nineteenth-century road engineers. Early car manufacturers often supplied just the engine and chassis and old-established firms of coachbuilders would add the body, custom-built to the specifications of a client. Thus they too moved into the garage business. In Somerset, a cycle shop proprietor and a coachbuilder

3

ABOVE: *James Fryer (right) was originally a coal merchant in Kington, Herefordshire, before turning to the cycle trade. His business expanded and he moved these to larger premises on the outskirts of the town.*

BELOW: *His premises altered, Mr Fryer (at the tiller of the car on the right - a curved-dash Oldsmobile Runabout) sold his first motor vehicle (a Beeston Humber tricycle) to a local doctor in 1899. He moved via motor cycles into car sales and repairs though, despite the impression given by this picture, he never learned to drive.*

In 1908 James Fryer moved his business to Hereford, twenty miles from Kington, forming a limited company in 1913. Between 1921 and 1922 this garage (photographed in 1949) was built. It covered 2,500 square feet and its brickwork matched that of the adjacent Boys' High School.

joined to form the Bridgwater Motor Company: an appropriate (if less common than might be supposed) combination which was managed by a pioneer motorist of the West Country, Harry Carver. Other traders also saw the possibilities of the motor vehicle and the telegraphic addresses in the first *Automobile Association Handbook* (1908) provide some clues: gunmaker; ironfounder; electrician; and several engineering firms (which had presumably gained a grounding in the principles of internal combustion from the oil engines then in use).

With this variety of origins, a name was needed for the new trade. The noun 'garage' originally meant the wide portions of French canals in which barges could dock or pass each other. It was appropriated by the French railways as a term for train sheds and, from this, was taken into French motoring terminology. Finally, in the company of several other French motoring words, it was imported into English; Frank Morris of King's Lynn, a former cycle agent, was probably the first provincial garage owner to describe his business as such. He did so in the spring of 1899, but he was very closely

followed by others, notably Daniel Albone of Biggleswade (Bedfordshire) and F. E. Bunting, who had 'Wealdstone Motor Garage' painted on his signboard in 1900.

The early garages were of necessity in county towns or large market towns. It was here that the gentry and the professional men, notably doctors, who were their customers might live. They had to be near railway stations because petrol, spares and even dismantled new cars in crates came by rail. In these towns, too, were locally generated electricity and the telephone. Consequently the shop-cum-garage became cramped with goods — even lawnmowers, sewing machines or phonographs might be on sale there — and, if there was a yard to the rear, that too filled up with vehicles, the high cars often difficult to negotiate through the narrow entrances.

Garage owners therefore began to have premises purpose-built for the trade. H. W. Egerton claimed that the company he formed in 1901 with G. N. C. Mann, with its premises at 5 Prince of Wales Road, Norwich, was one of the first all-motor sales, repair, storage and hiring businesses in Britain. Soon after-

5

Inside James Fryer's Kington garage. In the right foreground Jim Prothero, the foreman, is working on a 6 horsepower Wolseley. The garage was finally demolished in 1982, to make way for a new by-pass.

wards, in the early part of 1902, the Imperial Motor Works of Lyndhurst (Hampshire) was started. No garage business matched the rapid expansion of Mann Egerton. By 1913 its turnover had reached £300,000; it had sold over 3600 cars and had expanded into London.

The First World War curtailed building activity, but the first five years of peace revived the industry, as the table below indicates. Mass production of cars and the increased availability of oil widened the market for road transport and mass production of commercial vehicles (especially petrol tankers) freed it from dependence on the railway. In the country towns there was considerable competition for sites, with the tenancy of at least one garage being decided by the toss of a coin!

In the countryside, however, the increase in motor traffic encouraged the opening of garages. Because of the agricultural depression, land was cheap and space plentiful: the field perhaps at crossroads, outside a village or alongside a

year	private cars	motorcycles	buses, coaches and taxis	goods vehicles
1914	132,000	124,000	51,000	82,000
1919	110,000	115,000	44,000	62,000
1924	474,000	496,000	94,000	203,000
1929	981,000	731,000	98,000	330,000
1934	1,308,000	548,000	85,000	413,000
1939	2,034,000	418,000	90,000	488,000

This table shows the number of motor vehicles on the roads of Britain between 1914 and 1939. The information is derived from the 'Abstract of British Historical Statistics' by B. R. Mitchell and Phyllis Deane and the 'Second Abstract of British Historical Statistics' by B. R. Mitchell and H. G. Jones (both Cambridge University Press).

ABOVE: *H. W. Egerton was a considerable publicist for the car. He is shown here at Land's End in a Locomobile steam car, having driven it from John O'Groats — using 5 tons of water en route!*

BELOW: *A photograph taken in 1902 of one of the oldest garages in Great Britain — the Imperial Motor Works, Lyndhurst, Hampshire. The pitched roof was a feature common to several early garages — as was their storage of customers' cars.*

THE ROAD AGENCY SCHEME.

The Agent will display a small black flagstaff carrying a movable ball, painted *yellow*, with the letters **AA** in *black*.
On the lines of our Cyclist Patrols' Badge, this flagstaff when displayed thus—

The first AA handbook in 1908 listed 664 agents. These were appointed garages which also delivered messages to members, reported on road and traffic conditions and provided guides through towns. Communication to members was via this flagstaff system.

will mean

When displayed thus—

"I AM HERE IF YOU WANT ME."

it means,

"STOP, PLEASE! I HAVE SOMETHING TO REPORT."

In which case the Member's Badge or Card **must** be shown to the Agent.

busy road was sacrificed to the car.

In the 1920s there was little to hinder construction of garages or the new filling stations. The Automobile Association recognised demand for the latter and built the first at Aldermaston (Berkshire), followed by another seven in England. The oil companies saw the commercial possibilities and followed suit, as did other entrepreneurs. The innovation was not always welcomed. Some local authorities banned kerbside pumps, while others charged a rent for them. Furthermore, the increasing number of individuals and organisations concerned with protection of the environment took understandable exception to the eyesores which were frequently built.

Legislation appeared in the late 1920s. In 1927 the Roadside Petrol Pumps Act confirmed local authorities' power to license them and the Board of Trade's powers of inspection. In 1928 the Petroleum (Consolidation) Act outlined model bylaws, which county councils could adopt and enforce, governing the appearances of garages.

The discussion surrounding the Act and the bylaws illustrates the controversy over appearances. While firms of specialist garage constructors were emerging,

garages were very frequently the work of local builders, who seem to have followed loosely a cheap 'standard' plan of a portal frame of steel girders supporting a pitched or convex roof, with galvanised iron fixed to the frame. The galvanised iron was particularly disliked by the reformers. Bylaws ordered existing iron to be painted a suitable colour and that it be replaced in new constructions by a range of more substantial materials. Those recommended included, for the walls, bricks, clay tiles, timber framing and weatherboarding and, for the roof, natural slates, clay tiles again, and (rather dangerously) thatch. Before the bylaws garage owners had covered their premises with advertisements; now these were to be strictly controlled, with emphasis upon the unobtrusive informing of the motorist of a filling station and of the brand it sold.

Setting garages back from the highway, with a splay leading to them, was easier in theory than in practice; as representatives of the trade pointed out, many of Britain's thirty-six thousand garage proprietors did not have the capital to buy the necessary land, even if it was readily available adjacent to garage premises.

Environmental and architectural orga-

8

ABOVE: *The first AA filling station, built at Aldermaston in 1919. Manned by AA patrols, it was equipped with a 500 gallon tank (of benzole) and a hand-operated pump, air compressor, fire extinguisher and a supply of water.*

BELOW: *A plethora of signs being erected at Theale, Berkshire. The BP logo was designed by one of its employees in a competition held in 1920.*

Two examples of sign erection of which the Council for the Protection of Rural England (CPRE) took a dim view.
ABOVE: *Obtruding on the scenery on the approach to Burney, Leicestershire.*
LEFT: *A sign despoiling a tree near Stratford-upon-Avon.*

nisations held competitions to promote better designs. New garages and filling stations duly appeared, although some had a forced and exaggerated rusticity which was as repellent as the 'design' it supplanted.

Organised aesthetic opinion had failed to keep pace with business, for many garages and filling stations had been built before individual county councils drew up their bylaws. Unattractive many such garages may have been, but the modest corrugated iron sheds helped shape the future of rural Britain.

Examples of petrol-station designs which the CPRE considered commendable.
ABOVE: *In rustic style, at Oadby, in Leicestershire.*
BELOW: *In pagoda style, at Cheltenham.*

ABOVE: *A garage at Clun, Shropshire, photographed in 1937. Farm buildings erected after the Second World War adopted the same functional features typified here, the girder framework, the corrugated iron walls and the sliding door.*

BELOW: *A photograph redolent of the 1930s and illustrative of the 'ribbon' development which car-ownership helped encourage, in this case in Leicestershire.*

Hugh Thomas Hughes of Trawsfynydd, Gwynedd, established himself as 'cycle agent and repairer' in 1903, aged sixteen, and expanded this business into a garage before dying of war wounds in 1918.

THE EARLY GARAGE OWNERS

Since the garage industry combined different older trades into one new one, it is impossible to construct a picture of a typical garage-owner; one can, however, identify some features common to many of the pioneers.

Although the motorcar owes much to those aristrocrats who, like the Hon. C. S. Rolls, demonstrated its practicability, the cycle-shop owner or the coachbuilder who repaired it was of that honourable stratum of society the Victorians designated 'tradesman'. The garage owner was likely to be a nonconformist: Samuel Hicks, a Cornish blacksmith who progressed via a cycle shop to the establishment of a business which still bears his name, was a staunch Methodist. When the pioneers married, it was into families of their own class, so that close social and trading contacts were fixed.

Given such close connections, it is difficult to discover exactly from whom the early garage owner might have borrowed money or from whom he enjoyed long credit. Savings were the main source of capital; one garage owner in the south of England, for example, accumulated £140 with which to rent a shed and buy equipment. Enthusiasm, nevertheless, often outran both thrift and resources, so that many businesses were under-capitalised. Bolder spirits, however, were prepared to borrow and stake all they could on what they believed to be the rosy future of road transport. Sums well in excess of £2,000 were often spent on new premises in country towns by men who might allow themselves and their partners £2 or £3 per week as wages.

Confidence in one's own mechanical skills was therefore a prerequisite for the business and these skills were nurtured in coachbuilder's yard and cycle shop — and, indeed, outside them. Shop owners who turned themselves into garage owners were very frequently keen on cycling, as was W. J. Bladder, who founded a

13

ABOVE: *The cycle shop of Samuel Hicks in River Street, Truro.*
BELOW: *When Mr Hicks's business outgrew the River Street premises, a lease was taken out on this garage at nearby Boscawen Bridge, where coachwork and painting were done. This was also the depot for Ford's which, as part of the agency agreement, had separate premises.*

A bleak, midwinter setting to this photograph of a petrol station at Owler Bar, near Sheffield.

Worcester garage. Sometimes they were accomplished competitive cyclists, like the young Lord Nuffield. Building and repairing cycles, adjusting them to improve their performance, even patenting devices of value to the cyclist, as did Tom Norton, who founded the Automobile Palace in Llandrindod Wells, all were excellent practice. Breakdowns had to be repaired by practical men using their common sense and accumulated experience, often without recourse to a manual or assistance from the factory. The motorcar needed pioneer mechanics as well as pioneer drivers.

It was a young industry which attracted

An equally bleak, although misty, atmosphere surrounds this petrol station at Epsom — apparently under construction and possibly in operation.

HTP Motors garage, Truro, in the 1920s. HTP was originally a firm of agricultural merchants; Hosken, Trevithick and Polkinghorne (Trevithick was descended from Richard Trevithick, the locomotive pioneer). The firm became involved in garage business through the motor transport of agricultural goods.

the young, but successful business demanded more than mechanical knowledge, youth and enterprise. It demanded managerial ability; it demanded (often with the assistance of a hard-working wife) book-keeping skill and the social ability to move confidently among the car-owning classes. These were strenuous demands, yet the resources of the classes in trade in Edwardian times were sufficient to produce plenty of men and women who ably met them.

The garage business had grown considerably by 1914. The trade journal *The Garage* estimated then that annual tyre consumption amounted to £14,521,000, fuel and oil consumption to £8,500,000, and the cost of repairs to £6,000,000. It is estimated that half of this last figure was spent on wages and it also estimated the total wage bill of drivers and other hands to be £15,562,000. 'Liberty Day' was barely eighteen years before.

There were garage businesses in country towns which had become substantial and needed forms of organisation more appropriate than the partnership. 'Convert your business into a Private Limited Company!' advertised a London registration agent in 1914 and many garage owners took the advice both before and after the First World War. Indeed, by the Second World War some of the larger concerns were public limited companies.

The First World War diverted rather than stemmed the energies of the pioneers. Losing their workmen and materials to the war effort, they nevertheless found trade in the transport of wartime supplies and personnel; the newly founded Crosville garage turned bus company in Cheshire ran services to a munitions factory in Mold, for example. They found much trade, too, in the mechanisation of agriculture. (S. F. Edge, who had played a major part in the establishment of the British motor industry, was in 1917 appointed Controller of Agricultural Machinery in the Ministry of Munitions.) Tractor agencies were acquired during the war and retained after it, leading country garages into a new line of business. The work they did was recognised by the honouring of individuals, notably G. H. Butcher of James Fryer Limited, Hereford, who was awarded the MBE for his work in organising food production during the war.

Peace brought the coming of age of motor transport. There were doubtless

ABOVE: *The village garage at Bugle, Cornwall, in the mid 1920s. Parked outside it is a 1918 15 horsepower Swift Grey Torpedo tourer, a Rudge and two Douglas motor cycles, and a Ford Model 'T' car.*

BELOW: *The motor industry was one which attracted the young. Here five young men (four with their caps worn back-to-front in 'scorcher' style) pose on what may be a stripped down Darracq in a garage-yard at Presteigne (Powys).*

many who had been mechanics before the war and, like Bertie North in Miss Read's *The Market Square*, returned from the armed forces to 'the welcome routine of the motor trade'. But the promise of the industry brought new men into the countryside to start garages. Those who, during the war, had learnt to drive or the mechanic's trade used their gratuities to buy War Department lorries and start haulage businesses (building charabanc bodies on to the chassis to carry passengers). The switch from road haulage to garage owning was very easily made. Munitions workers, with savings and engineering skills, could start in the trade. Mechanically minded farmers' sons might join. Families disposing of their chauffeurs might set them up in the car-hire business, from which they could graduate to garages. The field was wide and the old nonconformist ties were shaken off.

Especially attractive to many were the new filling stations. 'The dream of operating a garage has replaced the country pub as the goal of many a man who wants a business of his own,' said a Services Resettlement Bulletin published much later in 1965. 'He knows a bit about cars, he's no mechanic but with his wife and a boy serving petrol round the front he reckons he could manage the odd grease-up . . . .' For those who could take the long hours and weekend work, who had a commercially viable station and the capital to offer a good service, the dream might in part come true. Other operators, lacking both capital and a prime site, fell on hard times as competition increased. The unsuccessful operator might then be forced to close down, leaving the filling station abandoned and derelict.

The effect of this rapid growth of small enterprises was the creation of a two-tiered garage industry in the countryside by 1939. In the county or market town there might be large garages with clerical, sales and workshop staff. These would hold the main car agencies and one or two might form parts of a national chain. In the villages and beside the busier roads were one-man concerns, small partnerships or family businesses. Between these tiers, however, there was a web of other businesses: road passenger and goods haulage, agricultural engineers and car-hire operators.

A photograph which appears to bely the statement that few small farmers in the north and west could have afforded new cars! An impressive display is parked outside this Welsh border garage; its owner, S. W. Brisbane, had also begun business with a bicycle shop.

Car hoist and high-pressure greasing plant at the Imperial Motor Works, Lyndhurst, in the late 1930s.

THE WORK OF THE COUNTRY GARAGE

The early garage owners who pioneered the trade had their work made more difficult by the lack of standardisation amongst motor manufacturers. Mass production, following the American example and with wartime urgency giving impetus to its adoption in Britain, conferred the blessings of standardisation upon both manufacturer and repairer. Nevertheless, there were probably sufficient non-standard vehicles in the countryside until well after the Second World War to call forth resourcefulness in garages.

'Mass production' implies 'mass market' and motor manufacturers moved further and further down market throughout the inter-war period. Car owners before 1914 tended to be wealthy and to have exclusive interests; garages were not commercially exclusive, for they undertook to obtain cars for their clients from any manufacturer. They also arranged delivery and a garage owner might enjoy an instructive trip to the factory to collect his customer's car. Sometimes it was difficult to distinguish between manufacturer and dealer in those days of custom-built coachwork, and watching coachbuilders at work then might also have illustrated that there is no clear line between past and present. They used skills generations old, of which perhaps the greatest was that of the varnisher, who banished everyone from his shop and laid the dust with water so that nothing marred the mirror-like finish demanded.

War curtailed car sales so that, immediately after it, there was a shortage of private cars so severe that pre-war cars sold second-hand at double their original purchase price. Garages attempted to

COMMERCIAL VEHICLES.

LEYLAND
(30 CWT - 12 TONS)

DURANT
(10 CWT)

S. P. A
(2 TONS & 2½ TONS)

REO
(25 CWT)

DAIMLER
(2½ - 3 TONS)

OVERLAND
(1 TON)

G & J
(1 TON - 5 TONS)

A display advertising commercial vehicle agencies in a west country garage.

meet this demand by manufacturing their own or by producing makeshift hybrids. However, when the boom broke in the winter of 1920-1 (driving many small manufacturers bankrupt), Lord Nuffield met the slump by dropping down what he called the 'pyramid of consumption'.

So successful was he in increasing his sales and his profits that his competitors were forced to follow suit. This was important to garages in five ways. Firstly, there was the multiplication of car sales; market-town garages invested in car showrooms and employed specialist salesmen. Secondly, the increase in new car sales created a wide-ranging second-hand market in which the village garage proprietor could dabble if he so chose. Thirdly, servicing and repair business

increased, which provided bread and butter work for all garages. Fourthly, the word 'exclusive' acquired a different shade of meaning when motor traders used it. To further its sales a motor manufacturer (with the example being set by the Ford Motor Company) would insist that a garage acted as agent for its models to the exclusion of all other manufacturers. Fifthly, this exclusivity, together with the availability of mass-produced, standardised, interchangeable spare parts meant that a market-town garage holding an agency would be expected to invest capital in an extensive range of them. In order to minimise its investment, yet satisfy its customers, the garage would have to recruit or train competent storekeepers.

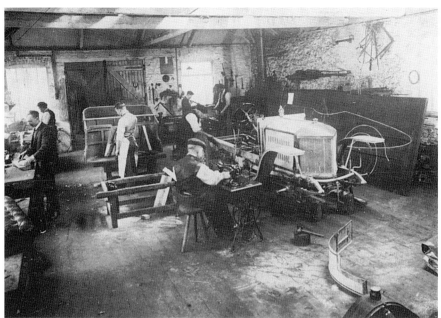

ABOVE: *The well equipped workshops of the Bridgwater Motor Company. The car is probably in the process of assembly from parts supplied by the manufacturer.*

BELOW: *The machine shop of the same company. Though lit by electricity, shafts, pulleys and belts were still required before the advent of small electric motors.*

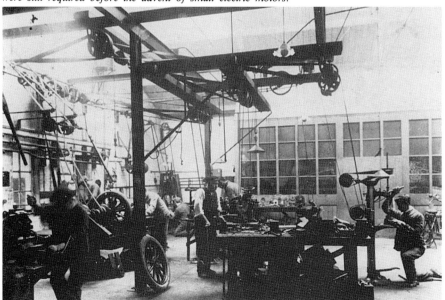

21

In spite of the price cutting of 1921 and 1922, rural poverty during the following twenty years restricted the sale of new cars to better-off country dwellers. Few small farmers in the north and west could have afforded even a small car and its depreciation — for example, the Standard Ten saloon was priced at £168 net in 1934 and in 1938 quoted at £57.

Second-hand cars might be bought for much less than £57, though. The salesman, earning around a basic £4 per week, might expect to sell a cheap one for two or three times his weekly wage and in 1932 a firm of used-car auctioneers advertised 'Good cars for one penny per pound'. Such auctions were becoming popular and in 1933 William Glass first published his *Guide to Used-Car Values*. Five years later the Society of Motor Manufacturers and Traders calculated that 38,070 cars more than ten years old were in regular use, a figure that perhaps indicates the extent of the second-hand trade. The countryman could possess a car if he so wished. Indeed, some writers on agriculture — Sir George Stapledon, for example — recommended the purchase of one for use as a cheap farm implement; this explains why modern restorers of vintage cars are able to find on farmland wrecks suitable for either cannibalisation or restoration.

Cars required constant replenishments of fuel, recoveries and repairs. Before 1914 the garage owner rolled springs, stitched upholstery, joined broken chains, replaced stretched belts, tightened up nuts which had worked loose and made new ones when they fell off and were lost. He stripped down cars and sent parts to the factory for repair, or he made the replacement parts himself. He filled lamps with carbide. He cleaned out fuel systems and wondered how he ought to spell 'carburettor' on the bill. He kept a forge, so that he could weld with brass; in 1909 a Gloucestershire garage charged one shilling for thus repairing two 'spaners' (sic) and fourpence for soldering a coffee strainer.

Most of all, he repaired punctures. Unsealed road surfaces and discarded horseshoe nails were the ruin of canvas and rubber tyres. The motorist carried a spare wheel (a 'Stepney wheel') which could be attached to the outside of the punctured one, thus enabling the journey to be continued. When he or she took the tyre in to be repaired, the cost of the job could vary from ninepence to three or four times that amount. Not surprisingly, such a variation made motorists indignant.

The other complaint they could make about pneumatic tyres was their short

There was little the earliest garages were not prepared to do, as this advertisement for a Shrewsbury garage in 1913 demonstrates.

ABOVE: *Tackle to cope with practically any accident or emergency and the recovery vehicle of the Bridgwater Motor Company. Note the apparently home-made ambulance jack, the cartwheels and axle, with a long pole to serve as drawbar.*
BELOW: *All the equipment could be stowed aboard the car, which, with a four-man crew, is shown turning out into Eastover.*

An advertisement for the Motor Owners' Petrol Combine Ltd. Aggrieved that oil companies sometimes bypassed them by supplying direct to certain customers, garage owners set up this company in an attempt to control the distribution to the retail trade.

life, about 6000 miles (9600 km). Cord woven into the rubber casing extended their life and this type of tyre had long been used by cyclists. In the early 1920s they were fitted as standard by the manufacturer, although most were imported. At the same time, arguments arose within the garage trade over their inflation. Should it be a free service or not? Larger garages decided it should be free and smaller ones had to fall into line. Ten years later garages large and small were losing the retail tyre trade to specialist firms.

There were still enough unusual models on the roads between the wars to call forth repairers' ingenuity and resourcefulness, although the readily interchangeable spares of the popular models cut down the time they were in the workshop. Nevertheless, whatever the model,

it required regular greasings, of some of its components more often than others. A motorist who valued his car might take it in for a monthly service and greasing: a West Country garage chain offered twelve such services for 3 guineas per annum.

The greasing bay was but one of the pieces of plant, purchased from the several firms now specialising in garage equipment, which was installed in country-town garages. Sophisticated equipment to test brakes or to wash with high-pressure water might be used there, as well as a hydraulic car hoist. The village garage owner used his inspection pit instead of the hoist and he accomplished most of the rest of his work with a range of hand tools, although he probably acquired gas cutting and welding equipment to assist him.

24

Saddest of all services was accident recovery work. The mayhem on the roads in the 1930s often brought mechanics out at all hours to tow in wrecks. For this was used an 'ambulance' jack, a two-wheeled towing jack which could be pushed under the crippled car to lever it off its own wheels and transport it away. Until the introduction of purpose-built recovery vehicles an extraordinary range of 'tow-cars' was used, of which the most remarkable was the Rolls-Royce which belonged to a Devon garage owner.

Fuel sales accounted for a proportion of the garage owner's turnover, if not always his profit. A wide variety of fuel was sold before 1914, including the coal-based benzole and several brands of oil-based motor spirit, of which the 'petrol' supplied by Carless, Capel and Leonard was but one. Fuel was transported by rail and in 2 gallon (9 litre) cans. Each company painted its cans a distinctive colour: those of Pratt's motor spirit, for example, were green. Garages fetched the fuel from goods yard depots, generally by horse-drawn dray, and stored it in cellars until it was sold.

Sales could bring difficulties, because cars' tanks were sometimes rather inaccessible or a customer might argue over the measurement of a partially full can.

The first kerbside fuel pump in Great Britain, installed by F. A. Legge outside his Betton House garage in Abbey Foregate, Shrewsbury. Garage owners also credited Legge with having installed the first electrically powered pump, a Xacto Bowser, in 1930.

More serious were the disputes between the trade as a whole and the oil companies. In 1914 garage owners justifiably complained that the price they paid for motor spirit left them with little or no profit margin (it retailed at 1s 3d a gallon, or 4.5 litres) and that the distribution system was clumsy and uneconomic. So bitter became the dispute that the trade set up its own distribution combine, the Motor Owners' Petrol Combine Limited, although wartime fuel shortages rapidly made these disputes a wry memory.

Pumps, which could measure out exact quantities of fuel from underground storage tanks, solved many distribution problems and the first roadside pump in Britain was installed in 1914 by F. A. Legge outside his garage in Abbey Foregate, Shrewsbury. Some garages started to follow his example straightaway,

although the main impetus came in 1919 from the Automobile Association's filling stations. The motor trade did not have the monopoly of the hand-cranked pumps: they also appeared outside village pubs, shops and even less likely places. In 1930 electric pumps started to replace the muscle-powered ones and, by 1938, there were in Great Britain a total of 98,100 pumps, each with an average annual throughput of 8,500 gallons (39,000 litres).

Profits from the country garage's petrol sales were always the product of a finely judged balance. The proprietor had to balance whatever credit he had from the oil companies or his bank against that which he gave his regular customers. He balanced the cost of hired labour against his profit margins and, if he used family labour, he balanced the ties he thus

An unusual place for a petrol pump was this one, installed in a gateway at the junction of a farm lane and a road, near Molland, Devon.

26

Crates of petrol cans stacked outside the first garage in Herefordshire, together with a De Dion motor car.

imposed on family life against the service he provided his customer.

All this was set against a background of falling petrol prices in the 1920s and fierce competition. In 1922, the year the BP refinery at Llandarcy began production, petrol was 2 shillings per gallon. In 1928, after severe price cutting, it was 1s 0½d.

Prices crept up again in the 1930s, although motorists protested vigorously at the tax they paid on each gallon (roughly half the retail price). When the Chancellor of the Exchequer, Sir John Simon, imposed another penny per gallon duty in 1938, taking the price up to 1s 7d per gallon, he provoked another outcry from the motoring interest. Their opposition was soon irrelevant, however, because within eighteen months war had been declared and petrol was rationed.

In 1903 the London Motor Garage Company Ltd advertised their new garage, with accommodation for two hundred cars, a lift to take them to each floor and even 'a chauffeur's room'.

28

Donald Healey, after being invalided out of the Royal Flying Corps, opened this garage in Perranporth, Cornwall, in 1917. On the extreme right is a Carden car, produced by one of the small car manufacturers of the 1920s, Carden Engineering Company, Ascot. Healey, after considerable success in car rallies, joined the Triumph Company in 1933.

A VARIETY OF REWARDS

The country garage was naturally the centre not only for the repair of most things mechanical, but also of mechanical transport.

Garage businesses had often started with car hire. 35 shillings a day (including driver) was a price quoted in Cornwall in 1911; nationally, the charge per mile varied around 9d. A shilling a mile was charged for an empty wedding car in Somerset in 1919, 1s 6d per mile with passengers. Hire of chauffeur-driven cars continued until the Second World War, although by then self-drive hire was emerging, with charges of 8d per mile. It is to be hoped that few early chauffeurs suffered the experience of an Imperial Motor Works employee, whose Amer-ican passenger in February 1914 drew a revolver on him and forced him to drive around the New Forest, occasionally demonstrating the gun's capability. The passenger committed suicide after his arrest.

Garages were the source of bus services and they repaired tractors and farm implements. A few establishments, notably the Automobile Palace in Llandrindod Wells, hoped for business from aeroplane sales and repairs but found themselves a little before their time. Goods haulage by road flourished, carrying coal, perhaps, or livestock, hop pockets, milk churns or sugar beet, although, with the lack of successful rural industries, business was liable to decrease

An advertisement for Pratts motor spirit, showing an idealised country garage blending in with its surroundings.

in winter. Some garages towed local fire engines; others carried the mail, as the Bridgwater Motor Company did between Bridgwater and Burnham-on-Sea from 1908 onwards.

Motor sport often claimed the interest of either garage proprietors — it could help sell vehicles — or the mechanics. Some made considerable names for themselves, for example Jimmy Guthrie, an ace motorcyclist until his accidental death in 1937, owned a garage in Hawick.

Repairs were not restricted to motor vehicles. The Gloucestershire garage which in 1909 soldered a coffee strainer fixed a new side on the vicar's lawnmow-

er three days afterwards. Moreover, in the days before the national grid, garages could provide electrical power, since some kept oil engines driving generators. (One Hampshire garage even utilised, via a waterwheel, a stream running under its premises). Local people could therefore bring in their accumulators to be recharged, to ensure that their wireless did not fade away, but, if the radio did break down, there was at least one village garage owner who could repair it.

The country garage probably helped speed up rural commerce, then typified in the annual settling up between farmer and corn merchant. The garage, with mortgages or rent payments to find and debts to oil companies and motor factors to meet, had to send its bills out and receive payment promptly. Those mentioned and pictured in this book were successful. There was a regular trickle of the most unsuccessful through the bankruptcy courts, with the oil and tyre companies the largest creditors.

What financial reward the proprietor of a village garage reaped from his hard work and his investment is difficult to estimate. A skilled mechanic in 1900 might expect to earn around a basic 25 shillings per week and this crept up to around 30 shillings when war broke out. If his son did the same job in the 1930s in a market town garage he might expect a basic £3 10s per week. There were undoubtedly at this time some one-man country garages where the owner paid himself less than the second-generation mechanic, except that the former attached a value to his independence.

Valuations of the businesses obviously vary greatly. In Kent a house and motor business described as 'lucrative' was offered at £2600 in 1938. In the same year a garage in the West Riding of Yorkshire, with living accommodation, four petrol pumps and space for ten cars, and situated at a crossroads, was advertised at £1400. This was at a time when a semi-detached house might be bought for between £250 and £550, depending upon the density of houses on its estate and the region of Britain in which it was situated. After the Second World War a garage and tea room (a popular combination), both in a fairly derelict condition, with a

30

poor bungalow, five hand-operated pumps and a small field, in Somerset, were bought for £5000.

When the Second World War came, the country garage felt its effects severely. Mechanics were lost to the war effort; transport was diverted to government requirements; fuel was in limited supply. Village priorities, however, remained high: the last job done in 1939 by the garage in Whitminster (Gloucestershire), was to thaw out the pipes in the village hall.

In the early days of motoring the customer might choose from a number of garages, even along the same street. This view of London Road, Hatfield, Hertfordshire (photographed about 1913) shows several garages. In the background is a cycle shop, with some men with bicycles standing outside. Next along the road is a garage advertising (among others) 'Motors for Hire', 'Vacuum Mobiloils' and 'Pratts Motor Spirit'; with another garage next to it (with a car parked on the forecourt). In the foreground is yet another garage, this one an agent for the AA and advertising Michelin products.

PLACES TO VISIT

Brooklands Museum, Brooklands Road, Weybridge, Surrey KT13 0QN. Restored clubhouse and various 1930s garages and workshops, including the BP petrol pagoda.
Telephone: 01932 857381. Website: www.brooklandsmuseum.com
Cotswold Motoring Museum and Toy Collection, The Old Mill, Bourton-on-the-Water, Cheltenham, Gloucestershire GL54 2BY. Period garage reconstruction.
Telephone: 01451 821255. Website: www.cotswold-motor-museum.co.uk
Heritage Motor Centre, Banbury Road, Gaydon, Warwick CV35 OBJ.
Telephone: 01926 641188. Website: www.heritage-motor-centre.co.uk
National Motor Museum, Beaulieu, Brockenhurst, Hampshire SO42 7ZN.
Telephone: 01590 612345. An extensive collection of memorabilia.
Haynes International Motor Museum, Sparkford, Yeovil, Somerset BA22 7LH.
Telephone: 01963 440804. Website: www.haynesmotormuseum.com

FURTHER READING

Bagwell, P. S. *The Transport Revolution since 1770.* Batsford, 1974.
Barty-King, Hugh. *The AA – A History of the First Seventy-five Years of the Automobile Association.* Automobile Association, 1980.
Boddy, Bill. *Vintage Motor Cars.* Shire Publications, 1990.
Demaus, A. B. *Victorian and Edwardian Cycling and Motoring.* Batsford, 1977.
Demaus, A. B. *Motoring in the Twenties and Thirties.* Batsford, 1979.
Ware, Michael. *A Roadside Camera.* David and Charles, 1974.
Ware, Michael. *Veteran Motor Cars.* Shire Publications, 1987.

ACKNOWLEDGEMENTS
When preparing this book in 1985 Llyn Morris acknowledged the help of a large number of people but especially his wife Vivien, Mr Basil Butcher of Hereford and Mr Michael Ware, curator of the National Motor Museum at Beaulieu. For this reprint, the publishers and Mrs Vivien Morris also acknowledge the assistance of Mr Harold W. Butcher, Mr A. Lloyd Hughes and Mr W. B. Watters.
Acknowledgement is also given to: Cambridge University Press, for permission to use statistics from the *Abstract of British Historical Statistics* by B. R. Mitchell and Phyllis Deane, and the *Second Abstract of British Historical Statistics,* by B. R. Mitchell and H. G. Jones; the Controller of Her Majesty's Stationery Office, for permission to quote from the *Services Resettlement Bulletin,* Number 11, (1965); Michael Joseph Ltd, for the use of the quotation from *The Market Square* by Miss Read.
Illustrations are acknowledged as follows: the Automobile Association, pages 8, 9 (upper); the late Mr Fisher Barham, page 17 (upper); the Bridgwater Motor Company Ltd, pages 21, 23; Mr John Brisbane, page 18; Mr Basil Butcher, pages 4, 5, 6, 7 (upper); Mr H. G. Edwards, page 12 (upper); Mrs E. M. Griffin (collection of the late Mr Claude Griffin), page 17 (lower); Mr M. M. Marriott, page 27; Mr John Mumford, page 20; the National Museum of Wales (Welsh Folk Museum), page 13; New Forest Services (Lyndhurst) Ltd, page 7 (lower), 19; the Royal Institution of Cornwall, pages 14, 16, 29; Shropshire County Library Service, page 25; University of Reading, Institute of Agricultural History and Museum of English Rural Life, pages 9 (lower), 10, 11, 12 (lower), 15.